The
ST NES

A Novel of the Life of KING DAVID

STUDY GUIDE

The ST◯NES

A Novel of the Life of KING DAVID

STUDY GUIDE

Eleanor Gustafson

THE STONES COMPANION GUIDE
By Eleanor K. Gustafson

Whitaker House
New Kensington, PA

The Stones Companion Guide

The Stones: A Novel of the Life of King David is a large book because David is a large and complex figure in biblical history. His personal life, at best, was up and down, and his participation in God's plan for the nation of Israel and beyond to the coming Messiah set him up for a closer and more frightening contact with *Yahweh* than he might have wished. I have prepared this Companion Guide to help sort out the convolutions of David's life. It is arranged in three major segments and can be used as a personal guide to the novel or for group study. I would encourage you to read the novel first, and then work through the guide.

I am not a Bible scholar, nor do I claim to be an expert on David or his role in the unfolding kingdom of God. Real scholars may take exception to some of my interpretations of the text and to the conclusions I have drawn. I can claim only a fascination for David that led me to scratch through every reference to and by him in my attempt to read his mind.

If you have a different take on David's life or further questions about either the book or about David himself, please contact me and we'll continue the conversation.

—Eleanor K. Gustafson
egus@me.com

Table of Contents

I. An Overview of David's Life and Assorted Personas

II. The People in David's Life

III. Heavy Matters

PHOENICIA

ZOBAH

Tyre

Damascus

Mt Herman

SYRIANS and ARAMAEANS

Abel Beth Dan
maacal

Geshur

TOB

Great Sea

Endor Chinnereth

meqiddo

Beth Shan Rogelim

mt. Gilboa Jabesh Gilead

mahanaim

Jabbok R.

Gibeon

Kirjath Gibeah
Jearim

Ashdad Socoh Nob Jericho
Adullam Gilgal
Bethlehem
Ashkelon Gath Keilah Jerusalem (Jebus) Rabbah

AMMON

Hebron
Ziklag Ziph En Arnon R.
PHILISTIA Gedi

Carmel

Beersheba

MOAB

EDOM

AMALEK

wilderness

Arabah

King's highway

Ezion-geber
(Elath)

An Overview of David's Life and Assorted Personas

1. Shepherd

In biblical times, the task of caring for sheep generally fell to children and to those not fitted for more demanding jobs.

- Joseph and his brothers were shepherds, as his mother had been before him.[1]
- David was out tending sheep when Samuel came to inspect Jesse's boys and anoint one of them as king.[2]
- Abigail first encountered David after a shepherd warned her of David's likely reaction on the heels of her husband's boorish behavior.[3]
- Doeg the Edomite, who murdered the priests of Nob, was Saul's head shepherd.[4]
- The prophet Amos identifies himself as a shepherd, as well as an orchardist caring for sycamore-fig trees.[5]

---

1. Genesis 29:6–9; 37:2
2. 1 Samuel 16
3. 1 Samuel 25:14–17
4. 1 Samuel 21:7; 1 Samuel 22:18
5. Amos 7:14–15

- The news of Jesus' birth was first proclaimed to shepherds—with an appropriate *"fear not."*[6]
- In the New Testament, shepherds were often lumped with gamblers, tax collectors, and other low life under the broad term of *"sinners."*

The Bible, however, clearly imparts new meaning to the term *shepherd,* using it as a redemptive metaphor.

- David was appointed by God to be the shepherd of Israel. Ezekiel said, *"I will place over them one shepherd, my servant David, and he will tend them; he will tend them and be their shepherd."*[7]
- Asaph, narrator of *The Stones,* wrote in one of his psalms,[8] *"He chose David his servant and took him from the sheep pens; from tending the sheep he brought him to be the shepherd of his people Jacob, of Israel his inheritance. And David shepherded them with integrity of heart; with skillful hands he led them."*
- Jesus, whom David prefigured, was the Good Shepherd.[9] And John speaks of him as both Shepherd and Lamb: *"For the Lamb at the center of the throne will be their shepherd; he will lead them to springs of living water. And God will wipe away every tear from their eyes."*[10]

God makes a point of using the concept of lowly shepherds to stand for something almost beyond our conceiving. Paul speaks of this upside-down aspect of God's economy. *"Brothers, think of what you were when you were called. Not many of you were wise by human standards; not many were influential; not many were of noble birth.*

---

6. Luke 2:8–20
7. Ezekiel 34:23. For a neat take on the job of shepherding, both good and bad, read Ezekiel 34 in its entirety. Psalm 23 also lines out the job nicely.
8. Psalm 78:70–72
9. John 10:14–15
10. Revelation 7:17

But God chose the foolish things of the world to shame the wise; God chose the weak things of the world to shame the strong. He chose the lowly things of this world and the despised things—and the things that are not—to nullify the things that are, so that no one may boast before him."[11]

David, the shepherd boy, was ready for great things.

Think for a moment:

1. What employment today would correspond to the job of shepherd in David's time?
2. Do you know of people today who started out in humble circumstances and later rose to prominence? Were they better or worse off for their experience?
3. How does Paul's word in 1 Corinthians 1:26 encourage or challenge you in your own circumstances?
4. How can we be more successful at resisting the pull of the world to "be somebody"?

2. Warrior (*gibbor*)

While the chronology of events as recorded in the Bible may be somewhat loose,[12] David initially appears to have come to King Saul's notice through his skill as a musical therapist. But when the boy felled Goliath, Saul saw him with new eyes and took him on as an armor bearer. An armor bearer, far from being simply a burden-bearing grunt, had to be fleet of foot and brain, one who could anticipate his boss's movements and the weapon he would need in any given situation. It was similar to being a good golf caddie.

---

11. 1 Corinthians 1:26–29
12. Saul's message to Jesse in 1 Samuel 16:22 seems to fit better at the end of chapter 17.

Saul promoted David to some sort of commanding rank in the army,[13] and the young man quickly became the heartthrob of the women of Israel and conversely, the target of the king's spears, even though Saul had benefited greatly from his chief warrior's victories over the Philistines. David continued to dodge spears until even his friend Jonathan, Saul's son, told him it was time to leave town.[14]

David then became the outlaw leader of a band of malcontents who lived by their wits and the generosity of landowners whose property they helped to defend. Saul pursued him relentlessly from mountain fortress to desert stronghold. Finally, in desperation, David offered himself and his men as mercenaries to the same Philistines he had fought so hard to defeat earlier. He mostly engaged in banditry against the Amalekites to the south of Judah, all the while building good will among the leading men of Judah. When Saul's military power began to implode, the Philistine king ordered David to go with him to the final battle. David was saved from having to fight Saul and Jonathan only when the Philistine generals began to have second thoughts about David's loyalty.[15]

After Saul's defeat and death, David became king, first of Judah, and then some years later of the whole of Israel. His army, headed by his nephew Joab and a cadre of extraordinary warriors (*gibborim*), was unstoppable, conquering all the surrounding nations. David fought in battles himself until he was nearly sixty, at which time his men drew the line—from then on, he would only be their lamp and not their warrior king.[16]

Early in David's career, the chief enemy of the Israelites was the Philistines who occupied the southwest Mediterranean coastland.[17]

13. 1 Samuel 18:5
14. 1 Samuel 20:42
15. 1 Samuel 29:6–7
16. 2 Samuel 21:15–17
17. See map on p. 8.

Their main cities were Ashdod, Gaza, Ashkelon, Gath, and Ekron, each governed by its "lord" or king. The period of their greatest strength came during the latter part of Saul's reign. David subdued them, but they continued to cause trouble for centuries until the time of Tiglath-pileser III, King of Assyria, in 734 B.C.

Another troublesome enemy was the Amalekite tribe that controlled the area to the south-southwest of Israel. When Moses led the Israelites from Egypt to the Promised Land, the Amalekites attacked them[18] and were defeated only with the help of Aaron and Hur who held up Moses' arms throughout the battle. *"Then the* LORD *said to Moses, 'Write this on a scroll as something to be remembered and make sure that Joshua hears it, because I will completely blot out the memory of Amalek from under heaven.' Moses built an altar and called it The* LORD *is my Banner. He said, 'For hands were lifted up to the throne of the* LORD*. The* LORD *will be at war against the Amalekites from generation to generation.'"*[19]

King Saul came to grief over Agag, the Amalekite king, after Samuel gave him specific instructions:

> *Samuel said to Saul,..."This is what the* LORD *Almighty says: 'I will punish the Amalekites for what they did to Israel when they waylaid them as they came up from Egypt. Now go, attack the Amalekites and totally destroy*[20] *everything that belongs to them. Do not spare them; put to death men and women, children and infants, cattle and sheep, camels and donkeys.'"*[21]

Saul did not do this but held back the best of the lot and spared the life of Agag the king. At that point, the search was on for a king to replace Saul.

---

18. Exodus 17:8ff
19. Exodus 17:14–15
20. See Stones Companion III, Heavy Matters, *Cherem.* p. 33
21. 1 Samuel 15:1–3

Other nations that David conquered include Edom, Moab, Syria, and the toughest of all—Ammon.

Psalm 18 is David's warrior song. In it he praises God for giving him the strength and talent to fight effectively. He was skilled with a sling (killing Goliath), could pull a bronze bow (the long-range weapon of the day), and was no slouch with sword and spear. Although the Philistines and other nations had horses and chariots, there is no record of David actually using them, especially on the hilly terrain of the area.

Work and *worship* have a common Hebrew root *(avodah)*. David, a consummate warrior (his work), gloried in his strength. In a real sense, war was a form of worship for David. He showed this by his passion in challenging Goliath's taunts against the God of Israel.[22] His worship didn't end there. War for David was not a matter of grabbing power and conquering nations; he devoted himself to setting things right as an instrument of justice and righteousness in God's hands. This was his calling; this was his life.

Think for a moment:

1. Why would Jesus, the "Son of David" and a Jew from the tribe of Judah, forbid His disciples from wielding the sword?
2. Can a Christian serve a combat role in the military or in domestic law enforcement?
3. At what point does a Christian switch from "turning the other cheek" to standing up to defend himself and others from injustice?
4. How can your work be an expression of worship and devotion to God?

---

22. 1 Samuel 17:45

3. Musician

David's musical ability is legendary. He made music in Saul's court to soothe the king's demons. The lyre he played was hand-held and like our modern-day harp only in that it had strings and a shape reminiscent of a harp. When David himself became king, music for worship was high on his agenda. Asaph, narrator of *The Stones*, was one of three chief Levite musicians that served at the Tent in Gibeon and in Jerusalem.[23] David, fixing his eye on the future temple that would be built by his son, developed the musical structure for temple worship.

David's poetry is well-known and loved. Seventy-three of the Psalms are attributed to him, and they express a wide range of emotions from awe to anger to vindictiveness to despair to trust and joy. He seems to have recorded life as it happened, for people to remember and use in worshiping God.

David often referred to God in metaphoric terms—David's fortress, his strong tower, a rock of refuge, his shepherd. He spoke of thirsting for God in a dry and weary land. He cried out in the warrior language of swords and shields and arrows, exhaustion and fear, as well as the euphoria of deliverance. In short, David wove the fabric of his poetry on the loom of everyday experiences. This was the world David knew, and he sang about it.

A number of psalms have specific musical instruction, such as, "*With stringed instruments. According to* sheminith." (Psalm 6) No one today knows what those terms mean, but Asaph would have known. He would also have been familiar with the tune, "*The Death of the Son*" as noted in Psalm 9. A sampling of musical notations appears in Psalms 4, 5, 8, 11, and others.

---

23. See Stones Companion II-2, Major Characters, Asaph.

Many psalms are intentionally connected with specific circumstances in David's life.

Psalm 3—When David fled from Absalom.

Psalm 7—Concerning his problem with Cush (Scroll One, chapter 11).

Psalm 30—Dedication of the temple. This one is tricky, in that the temple was built after David's death. He charged his son Solomon, *"Now, my son, the LORD be with you, and may you have success and build the house of the Lord your God, as he said you would."*[24] The psalm was probably written by David and used at the dedication.

Psalm 34—Feigning insanity before Achish (called Abimelech in this psalm heading).

Psalm 38—Labeled a "petition" and speaking of illness. In Scroll One, chapter 4, I created a wound sustained in Moab that fit the descriptive elements of this psalm. This is one of the few *"Help me!"* psalms that doesn't end on a note of praise and thanksgiving.

Psalm 51— Repentance over David's adultery.

Psalm 54—Ziphite betrayal.[25]

Psalm 56—Philistines seized him in Gath. This seems related to Psalm 34 and David's ploy of madness.

Psalm 63—In the harsh Judean wilderness.

Psalms 124, 131, 133—Songs of Ascent.[26]

Psalm 142—When David and his men hid from Saul in the cave.[27]

---

24. 1 Chronicles 22:11
25. In *Stones* Scroll One, chapter 11, I linked this to the problem with Cush mentioned in Psalm 7.
26. The Songs of Ascent were sung by processions of pilgrims making their way to the temple. The three Ascent psalms that are attributed to David may have been composed by him well before the temple was built and then used for this purpose at a later time.
27. 1 Samuel 24

Except for the Songs of Ascent, most of the labeled psalms start with cries of help or statements of need and end with a word of praise.

Musical instruments of David's day

- Trumpet—made of animal horns or metal and used in worship and for military signaling. It also signaled the new moon, the beginning of the Sabbath, and the death of a dignitary. Its musical capacity was limited; its primary purpose apparently to make noise.
- Flute—produced a high, shrill sound that, because of its association with fertility cults, was considered appropriate only in a secular setting to show both joy and sorrow.
- Harp or lyre—variously-sized, hand-held instruments of three to twelve strings.
- Lute—a small version of the harp or lyre, with only three strings.
- Timbrel—percussion instrument similar to a tambourine. It was played primarily by women and was not considered appropriate for worship, although they were used when the ark was brought to Jerusalem.
- Sistrum—rattling instrument with a U-shaped handle and pieces of metal or bone strung on bars, used often in mourning but sometimes in celebration.
- Cymbals—used in priestly functions and played only by men. They accompanied trumpets and other liturgical instruments. Asaph played the cymbals.

Think for a moment:

1. David's psalms have been the "praise songs" of countless generations. In our day, "worship" is often confused with the songs themselves. What constitutes genuine worship, especially when music is the "vehicle" for worship?
2. Muslims do not use music in worship because of its unholy associations in popular culture. Can music become a distraction to pure worship in our context? How can this be overcome?
3. On a scale of 1 to 10, taking into account the crude instruments of the day, rate Temple worship against the way your church leads worship. How about the singing of Jesus and his disciples and the early church? Today, when music or other parts of worship do not mesh well with our tastes, how can we learn to worship "by faith"?

4. Ladies' Man

I would not call David a womanizer. *Womanizing* implies "hookups" with multiple women. David had only one illicit relationship, but his collection of wives and "legal" concubines (one might call it "strategic polygamy") does suggest that were he living today, he'd be right up there. His affair with Bathsheba came while David was at the height of his powers. He had established his kingdom by defeating all of his surrounding enemies. He was King of the Hill, and according to the codes of the day, he could do as he pleased.

Bathsheba chose to bathe in plain sight near the palace. She probably thought that the king was off fighting the Ammonites with her husband Uriah and the rest of the troops. But David had chosen to stay at home, and in a moment of weakness he heeded his kingly privilege and desire. One sin follows another, and with the news of her pregnancy, murder followed adultery. Had Bathsheba not become pregnant, life might have gone on, one lapse spawning others. But ironically, in God's providence, Bathsheba did conceive, and far down the line the promised Messiah would come from that sinful union, but through another child.

Think for a moment:

1. Why do you think God chose Bathsheba, rather than a more "acceptable" wife (such as Abigail) to establish the House of David and the long line leading to the birth of Jesus?
2. What did Jesus have to say about such sins in the Sermon on the Mount? (Matthew 5–7) In what ways has the modern church gotten off track regarding sex and marriage?
3. What are some ways we can affair-proof our marriages, given the blatant temptations that bombard us daily?
4. In *The Stones*, Asaph was greatly affected by David's colossal sin. (See Scroll Two, chapter 18). What, beyond the armband and scroll that David brought to him, restored his relationship with David?

5. Lover of God

What sort of spiritual instruction did the child David receive? David grew up during the days of Samuel, the last of the judges and an "in-your-face" prophet. David's family tree included his Moabite great-grandmother Ruth and her godly Hebrew husband Boaz. Jesse's family probably worshiped *Yahweh* happily. And judging from David's spiritual passion, we know Jesse's training must have sent roots deep into the fertile soil of the boy's heart.

Spirit-filled – We don't know how old David was when Samuel anointed him to replace Saul, but we're told[28] that the Spirit of the

---

28. 1 Samuel 16:13

Lord came on him mightily from that day on. When David stood up to Goliath,[29] he must have been in his mid-teens, but he had a clear grasp of who God was, who the Israelites were as God's special people, and the nature of the Philistine army. *"Who is this uncircumcised Philistine that he should defy the armies of the living God?"*[30] Nor did David lack chutzpah, saying, in effect, "Hey, guys. I'm here. Don't worry about the giant; I'll take care of him."[31] David had experienced God's protection through his years of shepherding. Could a giant be any greater challenge than rescuing a sheep from the jaws of a bear or lion?[32] In this moment of David's God-ordained destiny, he faced the giant with fire in his belly. *"You come against me with sword and spear and javelin, but I come against you in the name of the* Lord *Almighty, the God of the armies of Israel, whom you have defied."*[33] He was physically and spiritually prepared, and he made good on his boast by felling Goliath with a stone and beheading him with the giant's own sword.

Subject to God's will – During David's years of running from the insanely jealous King Saul, David never took matters into his own hands, even when he had seemingly God-given opportunities to do so. *The Stones* relates David's close encounter with Saul in a cave in the barren hills west of the Dead Sea.[34] On another occasion, David could have driven a spear through Saul while he slept but refused. *"As surely as the* Lord *lives, the* Lord *himself will strike him; either his time will come and he will die, or he will go into battle and perish. But the* Lord *forbid that I should lay a hand on*

---

29. 1 Samuel 17
30. v. 26
31. v. 32
32. 1 Samuel 17:34–37
33. v. 45
34. 1 Samuel 24; Scroll One, chapter 11

the LORD*'s anointed.*"[35] Even after Saul was killed in battle,[36] David continued to honor him and executed the Amalekite who bragged about his hand in Saul's death.[37] David commended the men of Jabesh Gilead who retrieved the bodies of Saul and Jonathan and gave them proper burial.[38]

Returning the Ark – After David had been made king of both Judah and Israel, his first task was to bring the Ark of the Covenant to a place of honor in Jerusalem. Years earlier, it had been captured by Philistines who found it too hot to handle. They returned it, and for years it sat at the home of the Levite Abinidab in Kirjath-jearim until David made a place for it, probably on his palace grounds,[39] with Abiathar as high priest. The main tabernacle remained at Gibeon, with Zadok as chief priest.

While Psalm 132, a Song of Ascents, is not ascribed to David, it powerfully reflects his desire to find a place for the ark. It took two tries to get it there,[40] but David worshiped before the Lord, leaping and dancing *"with all his might."*[41]

Plans for the temple – David's next priority was to build a temple for the LORD.[42] Nathan the prophet thought it a great idea, but God had a different word for David, saying, in effect, "No, you have too much blood on your hands to build me a house. That's a task for your son. Instead, I'll build your house and make your name great, like the names of the greatest men of the earth. Your throne will be established forever." Read David's response to this covenant

35	1 Samuel 26, esp. 10–11
36	1 Samuel 31
37	2 Samuel 1:6–10
38	1 Samuel 31:11–13; 2 Samuel 2:4–7
39	See 2 Chronicles 8:11
40	See *Stones* Scroll Two, chapter 6
41	2 Samuel 6:14
42	2 Samuel 7

in 2 Samuel 7:18–29. This was a man whose heart was totally fixed on *Yahweh*.[43]

Sin effect – That, however, was before Bathsheba. During the long war with the Ammonites,[44] David's appetites got the best of him. He sinned with great abandon, breaking the seventh and sixth commandments (in that order). [45] But though he sinned fervently, he also repented fervently,[46] which set him apart, not only from Saul, but also from other kings of that era who did whatever they liked with whomever they wished without a second thought.

After Nathan's rebuke,[47] the consequences began almost immediately: the illicit baby died, David's son Amnon raped his half-sister Tamar,[48] Tamar's brother Absalom murdered Amnon,[49] Absalom led a rebellion against his father David,[50] and Sheba turned Israel against the cursed king.[51]

David's counting of his fighting men[52] has traditionally been looked on as a sin of pride, and 1 Chronicles 21:1 categorically states it was Satan-inspired. Asaph and I have cast it somewhat differently, though David himself said to God, *"I have sinned greatly by doing this. Now, I beg you, take away the guilt of your servant. I have done a very foolish thing."* [53]

---

43. Read about the Davidic covenant in Isaiah 55:3, 4, with the whole of the chapter as background. The Apostle Paul comments on this passage in Acts 13:34ff.
44. 2 Samuel 10–12; see also 1 Chronicles 19, 20
45. 2 Samuel 11–12; *Stones* Scroll Two, Chapter 14–17
46. See Psalm 51
47. 2 Samuel 12
48. 2 Samuel 13; *Stones* Scroll Three, chapter 4
49. 2 Samuel 13:23ff; *Stones* Scroll Three, chapter 8
50. 2 Samuel 15–17; *Stones* Scroll Three, chapters 13–20
51. 2 Samuel 20; *Stones* Scroll Three, chapter 23
52. 2 Samuel 24; *Stones* Scroll Three, chapters 24, 25
53. 1 Chronicles 21:8

David's heart, God's heart – David's theology shows up vividly in his life and psalms. God is not only Creator,[54] he is an all-powerful defender,[55] one who cares and provides,[56] who is just,[57] and a God of grace and mercy[58]—to name just a few of his attributes.

The last words of David, as recorded in 2 Samuel 23, show his life-long devotion to *Yahweh*, the God of Jacob: *"Is not my house right with God? Has he not made with me an everlasting covenant, arranged and secured in every part? Will he not bring to fruition my salvation and grant me my every desire?"*[59] David was indeed a man after God's own heart, and this comes to light most vividly in the context of his most sinful act and subsequent humility.

Think for a moment:

1. How does David's obsessive loyalty to Saul show his devotion to *Yahweh?* How would you have responded to the "God-given" opportunities to kill Saul?

2. What, according to Asaph, prompted David to assess the strength of his troops? Read Scroll Three, chapter 24, carefully.

3. As intimated in the last sentence of the preceding paragraph, how can a person's sin ultimately bring pleasure and even glory to God?

4. In what ways do we diminish our whole-hearted devotion to God in our relationships, our workplace, our churches, and our dealings with the world?

---

54. Psalms 8 and 19
55. Psalms 18 and 21
56. Psalm 23
57. Psalm 35
58. Psalms 51 and 103
59. 2 Samuel 23:5

6. King

The nation of Israel was a theocracy (rule directly by God) until they fell away, and a long line of judges, good and bad, made the people clamor for an earthly king.[60] Both God and Samuel spelled out for them the downside of a king.[61] God finally gave his assent and singled out the imposing but socially awkward Saul for Samuel to anoint. Saul and his son Jonathan performed well for a while under God's direction, but then Saul began to take matters into his own hands, responding badly to his "God-given" opportunities (see question 1 on p. 23). He didn't wait for Samuel's arrival to do the required sacrifices,[62] and most egregiously, he failed to finish off all the Amalekites as God had ordered.[63] Samuel loved Saul, and though he refused to see him again, he continued to mourn the king's failure.

1 Samuel 16 tells the story of David and his anointing. Saul began to unravel about this time, and David was pressed into service to soothe the king's inner demons.[64]

All of this happened before Goliath appeared on the scene and put Saul and the Israelites in a panic. David was perhaps a year or two older by now but still only a boy and still going back and forth between watching his father's sheep and displaying the medicinal

---

60. Read Judges 2:8–19 to get the whole sorry picture of why these judges were necessary.
61. Read 1 Samuel 8:10–18 for their take on kings. Chapters 9 and 10 tell of God's choice and Saul's anointing.
62. 1 Samuel 13:7–14
63. 1 Samuel 15. At some point, refer to III of this guide and the discussion of *cherem*.
64. Read 1 Samuel 16:14–23. One can only speculate about the psychiatric disorders Saul was prone to. Depression? Bi-polar behavior? He certainly suffered from paranoia with his baseless pursuit of David.

properties of harp music. David knew he had been anointed king but was simply waiting for Saul to grow old or die in battle.

David's victory over Goliath changed that—for better and for worse. With Goliath dead, Saul took note of this young headache remedy whom he had known only as a soothing presence in a dark corner of his bedroom. Now Saul saw David's military potential and wanted the boy to say goodbye to sheep and stay with him at the palace. He soon made David a commander—a move popular not only with the troops, but also with women who cheered and danced and sang,

> Saul has killed his thousands, and David his ten thousands.[65]

This adulation did not play well with Saul; from then on, everything went downhill for David.

After Saul's death, David still had to solidify the blessing of the leaders of Judah. In Israel, tribes made a king. David could not simply say that Samuel had anointed him years ago and then strong-arm his way to the throne. (Late in David's life, after Absalom's rebellion had been put down, he had to wait until the leaders of Judah made up their minds about reinstating him.)[66] After Saul's death, God instructed David where to establish his throne, and there in Hebron, he was finally crowned king.[67]

While only the King—but only of Judah, David still had to deal with the remains of Saul's monarchy: Saul's son Ishbosheth, his general Abner who established Ishbosheth's throne, plus ten cranky tribes who wanted nothing to do with David. The struggle went on for seven years until Joab murdered Abner and two of Ishbosheth's

---

65. 1 Samuel 18:7
66. 2 Samuel 19:11–12
67. Scroll One, chapter 18

captains assassinated their king, hoping for a reward from David.[68] By this time the tribes of Israel had decided that David was the legitimate king, after all,[69] and he was again crowned as monarch over all of Israel. After moving his throne from Hebron to Jerusalem, David brought the Ark of God there, thus establishing an impregnable position—physically, politically, and spiritually. Finally, he was God's man on the throne.

Think for a moment:

1. In what ways did Saul and David differ as monarchs?

2. Drawing from Scripture and from material in *The Stones*, what conditions were necessary for a monarchy such as David's to be established? Read Jeremiah 23:5–6 and other passages in III-3 of this guide.

3. What should be our attitude and role in local and national affairs—as individuals and as a church? (Cf. 1 Timothy 2:1–3, 8; Matthew 22:21; 1 Peter 2:13–14)

---

68. See *The Stones*, pp. 213–15

69. Most likely by the eating of salt. In *The Stones*, you may have noticed the phrase, "covenant of salt" or "eating bread and salt." This refers to the ancient practice of ratifying both friendship and treaties through the ritual use of salt. 2 Chronicles 13:5 states it plainly: *"Don't you know that the Lord, the God of Israel, has given the kingship of Israel to David and his descendants forever by a covenant of salt?"* Salt was mandated for Levitical sacrifices, as well. Even today, Arabs use the same word for salt as for treaty.

People in David's Life

1. A word about Hebrew pronunciation:

As you look at all the people names in this section, you may be tempted to start flipping pages. Big kings and their kingdoms generally involve a lot of people, but you may find some fun in learning to pronounce these names. Simple pronunciation of transliterated Hebrew is not hard to master. The letter A is always pronounced *ah*, E is always *eh*, I is always *ee*, O is always *oh*, and U is *oo*. David, then, would be pronounced *Dah-VEED*. Benaiah would be *Ben-AH-ee-ah*. Baal would be *Bah-ahl*, separating the syllables. Absalom's mother Maacah would be *Mah-ah-cah*. Abigail is actually spelled *Avigail* but, as v sounds like b, it is pronounced *Ah-bee-gah-eel*. Try a hard one, David's son Beeliada. And rethink some Bible book pronunciations, like Isaiah or Daniel.

2. Family connections

Some dry stuff here, but you need to get these people sorted out. David belonged to the tribe of Judah (fourth son of the patriarch Jacob and his wife Leah). David's immediate ancestors were Salmon, his son Boaz (who married Ruth the Moabite), their son Obed, and David's father Jesse. Jesse's seven sons were Eliab, Abinadab, Shimea (father of Jonadab, Amnon's conniving friend), Nethanel, Raddai, Ozem, and lastly, David—a strong, handsome bunch. David had two notable sisters: Zeruiah, who birthed Abishai, Joab, and Asahel; and Abigail (not to be confused with David's wife Abigail), whose son was Amasa, Absalom's general.

These are David's wives and children:

Michal, daughter of Saul	Abital
Ahinoam	Shephatiah, son
Amnon, son	Eglah
Abigail	Ithream, son
Daniel, son, also called Kileab	Bathsheba
Maacah	(Boaz), son
Absalom, son	Solomon, son
Tamar, daughter	Nathan, son
Haggith	Shobab, son
Adonijah, son	Shammua, son

The mothers of the following children are not specified:

Ibhar	Japhia
Elishua	Elishama
Elpelet	Beeliada
Nogah	Eliphilet
Nepheg	Jerimoth

Solomon was chosen by God to carry along the line of David that led directly to the Messiah.[70]

3. Major characters

An author of biblical fiction must walk carefully. What does the Bible actually say about the characters, and what can be inferred?

---

70. See the genealogies of Jesus as listed in Matthew 1 and Luke 3. They are not identical, in that Matthew traces the line of Joseph and Luke traces Mary's line.

For the finished product to convey the true meaning and purpose of Scripture, an author's intuition and imagination must fit well with what is known or clearly implied. This I have tried to do.

We know most about **David**, of course, because we find more about him in Scripture than about any other biblical character except Jesus. Nevertheless, I have embellished. I fleshed out relationships with wives and Mighty Men. I gave David quirks, such as eye blinking in his later years. In short, I plumped up his personality.

The Stones is nearly as much about David's nephew **Joab** as it is about David. Joab is clearly a loathsome character, and David clearly despised him. See the question following this section on why David put up with him.

David's third wife **Abigail** is one of my favorite characters. You can read her story in 1 Samuel 25. There she is described as capable, enterprising, devout, and attractive to David's eye. To these characteristics I added "principled," creating a tension in *The Stones* that marks their entire relationship. Abigail's love for David was deep and powerful, but that too was often misunderstood.

Bathsheba stands out in everyone's mind, and she played a critical role in David's life—for better or for worse. Despite her complicity in David's sin, God did appoint her son Solomon to succeed David and to carry the seed of his line. There's too much of Abigail in me to approve of that, but then, my ways are not God's ways.

Benaiah, chief of David's bodyguard, plays a major part in the biblical story, but little is known about him.[71] Though not noted in *The Stones*, one of Solomon's first acts as king was to replace Joab with Benaiah as commander-in-chief.[72] I crafted Benaiah as a

---

71. Read 2 Samuel 23:20–23
72. 1 Kings 2:35. At the same time, Solomon also replaced Abiathar, David's high priest, with Zadok.

skilled *gibbor* who was loyal, easy to work with, and an honorable person. At one point, David wished he were one of his own sons.

Hushai does not appear in Scripture until David is leaving town in a hurry to elude Absalom's takeover of the throne.[73] Hushai then plays a key role in David's escape.[74] There is one other reference in 1 Chronicles 27:33, where it says, *"Ahithophel was the king's counselor. Hushai the Arkite was the king's friend."* I expanded on that, giving Hushai a history and prominence as the king's friend. I like him very much. Any friend of David's is a friend of mine.

Ahithophel was indeed a superb counselor. Second Samuel 16:23 remarks, *"Now in those days the advice Ahithophel gave was like that of one who inquires of God. That was how both David and Absalom regarded all of Ahithophel's advice."* He was also the father of one of David's Mighty Men, Eliam, the father of Bathsheba, making Ahithophel Bathsheba's grandfather.[75] Ahithophel was wise and expected to be listened to. When Absalom followed Hushai's advice instead of Ahithophel's, the latter saddled his donkey, put his affairs in order, and hanged himself.[76]

At least three of David's sons—Amnon, Absalom, and Adonijah—were outright disasters. (See questions.) We know nothing from Scripture about Abigail's son **Daniel** except the absence of his name as a possible successor of David. I have constructed him out of pure imagination, blending the (imagined) attractiveness of Bathsheba's firstborn with the (known) intellect of Solomon. Daniel, at least as I created him, is another person I would like to meet.

Abiathar succeeded his father Abimelech as high priest after Saul's slaughter of the priests at Nob.[77] I shaped him as I did, largely to

---

73. 2 Samuel 15
74. See *The Stones*, Scroll Three, chapter 16
75. 2 Samuel 23:34; 2 Samuel 11:3
76. 2 Samuel 17:23
77. 1 Samuel 22:6ff

fit his spineless defection to Joab in the latter's attempt to enthrone Adonijah instead of Solomon. **Zadok**, the chief priest who served at the Tent in Gibeon, seems much stronger,[78] and Solomon did in fact draft him to replace Abiathar as High Priest.

And of course, **Asaph**. Although only a minor player in the actual story, his presence and outlook on each turn of events lends its own light to the narrative.

Asaph is somewhat more than just a name in Scripture. See 1 Chronicles 6:31ff for the three major court musicians—Heman, Asaph,[79] and Ethan—complete with their genealogies. 1 Chronicles 15:16–22 lists the musicians involved in bringing the Ark to Jerusalem. The following chapter speaks of Asaph as one of the chief musicians[80] and lines out the psalm of thanks that David committed to him and his associates.[81] A number of psalms are attributed to Asaph, scattered between Psalm 50 and 83, and he evidently established a school of music, referred to in Ezra 3:10 as *"the sons of Asaph."* 1 Chronicles 25:2 refers to Asaph as one who *"prophesied under the king's supervision."*

To reflect all of these factors, I gave him a fussy, detailed personality that serves him well as an historian. I also cast him as sensitive, with a jealous longing in his heart for a close friendship with the king.

Among the lesser characters, **Obil** the camelmaster is high among my favorites. I discovered him in one of the dry lists of army divisions, officers of the tribes, and the king's overseers in 1 Chronicles 27. He gets brief mention in verse 30—*"Obil the Ishmaelite was in*

---

78. 1 Chronicles 12:28 indicates that the Levite Zadok, who joined David in Hebron, was a warrior.
79. 1 Chronicles 6:39
80. 1 Chronicles 16:5
81. 16:7ff. Snatches of this praise song can be found in Psalms 105:1-15; 96:1–13; 106:47–48.

charge of the camels." That's it. But it caught my eye, and my imagination took off from there. He pops up throughout the story and saves the day in the final battle.

Think for a moment:

1. Why didn't David lop off Joab's head after the latter murdered Abner? Was Joab a necessary tool in *God's* redemptive plan? Is Joab's brother Abishai equally culpable? (See 2 Samuel 23:18, 21:17, 16:5–12, and 19:21–22.)

2. If Abigail is David's most valuable wife, why is he uncomfortable with her? In what way does Abigail exemplify God's love?

3. In Scroll Three, chapter 17, Ahithophel blames his own poor judgment for Hushai's advice trumping his own. What particulars had he missed? Why does he envy Hushai, and what does that tell you about Ahithophel himself?

4. What were Absalom's leadership characteristics? What factor(s) worked to bring about his downfall? What was the principle difference between him and his father?

5. The components of effective leadership are a major topic of discussion in today's world. What useful insights can we gain from studying the diverse characters in *The Stones?*

6. Who are the significant players in your life story? Do any of them parallel the people surrounding David? The people of God have always been a mixed lot, with strengths and weaknesses showing up as we grow into the likeness of Jesus. Does this challenge you or give you hope?

Heavy Matters

1. Cherem and the fear of God

As noted in the preface of *The Stones*, the concept of *cherem*, the God-ordained practice of wiping out men, women, children, and livestock, and devoting the carnage to God, is a sticky issue. Leviticus 27:28 says, *"But nothing that a man owns and devotes to the Lord—whether man or animal or family land—may be sold or redeemed; everything so devoted is most holy to the Lord."* The NIV footnote adds, "The Hebrew term refers to the irrevocable giving over of things or persons to the LORD."

Other passages that refer to this practice include Numbers 18:14, where God instructs Aaron in priestly duties and privileges: *"Everything in Israel that is devoted to the Lord is yours"*, and Joshua 6:17: *"The city and all that is in it are to be devoted to the Lord. Only Rahab the prostitute and all who are with her in her house shall be spared, because she hid the spies we sent."*[82]

One commentator ties the total destruction of Jericho not only to the sinfulness of its inhabitants, but also to this particular city being the firstfruits of the conquest of the land promised to Abraham.

---

82. See also Numbers 21:2, Deuteronomy 2:34, Judges 21:11.

"God is teaching Israel that they must be grateful and give Him the firstfruits of whatever they have.[83] As such, everything in it must be dedicated to the Lord; the perishable to the flames, and the imperishable to the Lord's treasury. As such, nobody is allowed to take any of the livestock or goods from the city as booty. Those who do so are subjected to the same treatment given to the inhabitants of Jericho, as Achan found out to his and his family's destruction (Joshua 7:10–26)."[84] King Saul also came to grief over this issue.[85]

Another website points out the wickedness of the Cannanites who inhabited the Promised Land. "[They] were not, as some imagine, innocent people minding their own business, living peaceably in the Land. They had completely given themselves over to idol/devil worship and paganism (see 1 Corinthians 10:19–20), and their society was totally corrupt. For instance, one of their common practices was to burn alive their newborn babies in a sacrificial fire to their demon gods. These were wicked people, and God did not want his people Israel to be led astray to other 'gods' and their practices. (See Leviticus 18:21; Psalm 106:37)."[86] Unfortunately, going astray happened often in Old Testament history. God is just, as we see in these passages, but he is also love, as we see in his protection of Rahab in Jericho who aligned herself with God's people.

Think for a moment:

This issue should generate some conversation.

1. What are your thoughts concerning *cherem*? Try to argue both sides of the issue.

---

83. Deuteronomy 26:1–11
84. Daniel Chew's blog post:
    http://puritanreformed.blogspot.com/2007/11/on-concept-of-cherem.html
85. Read 1 Samuel 15
86. http://wordofmessiah.org/june_05_3.htm

2. *Jihad* is the Islamic version of *cherem*. Why is *Jihad* "wrong" and biblical *cherem* "right"?

3. How do you look at capital punishment in our day?

4. God always warns people before executing judgment. What warnings do we see in our own day, and how are they being heeded in our own lives, in our church, and in our nation?

This brings up another topic: **The fear of God.** We have little concept today of what it means to truly fear God. We don't even like to use the word. We turn *fear* into "awe" or "wonder" or "reverence." Check out the praise songs we sing. How often does the word *fear* occur? Somehow, we think that fear belongs strictly to the Old Testament and is not appropriate to the New. If this is your approach, you might read John's physical reaction to his vision of the Alpha and the Omega, the First and the Last, in Revelation 1:17–18. Here are some other New Testament verses on the fear of God—each with my emphasis added:

- Acts 9:31 – "*Then the church throughout Judea, Galilee and Samaria enjoyed a time of peace. It was strengthened; and encouraged by the Holy Spirit, it grew in numbers, living in the **fear of the Lord.**"*

- 2 Corinthians 5:11 – "*Since, then, we know what it is to **fear the Lord**, we try to persuade men. What we are is plain to God, and I hope it is also plain to your conscience.*"

- Philippians 2:12–13 – "*Therefore, my dear friends, as you have always obeyed—not only in my presence, but now much more in my absence—continue to work out your salvation **with fear and trembling**, for it is God who works in you to will and to act according to his good purpose.*"

- 1 Peter 2:17 – "*Show proper respect for everyone: Love the brotherhood of believers, **fear God**, honor the king.*

- Hebrews 10:30–31 – "*For we know him who said, 'It is mine to avenge; I will repay,' and again, 'The Lord will judge his people.' It is a dreadful thing to fall into the hands of the living God.*"
- Revelation 15:4 – "*Who will not fear you, O Lord, and bring glory to your name? For you alone are holy. All nations will come and worship before you, for your righteous acts have been revealed.*"

And perhaps the most compelling example in the New Testament:[87] "*Great fear seized the whole church and all who heard about these events*" after God struck down Ananias and Sapphira. Wanting the praise of men as well as a portion of the money they "devoted" to the church, they connived and lied. And God acted. No one in church that day would have even considered defining *fear* as merely "reverent awe."

David was terrified of God—and for good reason. Consider the death of Uzzah after he inadvertently touched the Ark. Remember Nathan's rebuke after David's affair with Bathsheba. In Scroll Three, chapter 1, David stands up to Abigail's indignation over the prophet Gad's remedy for the famine brought on by an old injustice to the Gibeonites. Seven of Saul's descendants would have to die. David says to Abigail,

> It's bloodguilt, and the entire nation is suffering. Can't you see that? I've got to do whatever is necessary to stop the suffering. I can't countermand God's order. You of all people should understand that. You didn't watch Uzzah explode just for trying to protect the ark. If you had seen it, Abigail, you'd have been every bit as angry as I was. *I don't understand God, Abigail. I don't understand, but I must obey.*

---

87. Acts 5:1–11, emphasis added

At the end of Scroll Three, chapter 25, David is given two glimpses behind the veil of time and space—first when he sees the angel of death over Jerusalem,[88] and second, when the fire of God consumes his offering on Araunah's threshing floor.[89]

Yes, David knew well this God who is to be feared!

When God gave the Law to Moses at Sinai, the whole mountain seemed ready to come down on the people.[90] Moses told the terrified people, in effect, "Don't be afraid. Yes, you need to fear God because healthy fear will help keep you from sinning."[91]

God is holy, and we need to understand what that means, especially in relation to his love and grace and mercy. After all, Jesus did instruct us to address God as "our Father." We are comfortable with love and grace; we could do without the holy part. Mike Yaconelli says it this way:

> I would like to suggest that the Church become a place of terror again; a place where God continually has to tell us, "Fear not"; a place where our relationship with God is not a simple belief or a doctrine or theology, it is God's burning presence in our lives. I am suggesting that the tame God of relevance be replaced by the God whose very presence shatters our egos into dust, burns our sin into ashes, and strips us naked to reveal the real person within. The Church needs to become a gloriously dangerous place where nothing is safe in God's presence except us. Nothing—including our plans, our agendas, our priorities, our politics, our money, our security, our comfort, our possessions, our needs.[92]

---

88. 1 Samuel 24:15–17

89. 1 Chronicles 21:26

90. Exodus 19:16–19

91. Exodus 20:20, loose paraphrase

92. http://www.acts17-11.com/fear.html. The original was published in The Wittenburg Door, Issue #131, September/October, 1993.

Think for a moment:

1. The faithful people of Narnia who knew Aslan were quick to say, "He is not a tame lion." Would David agree with this? Do you?

2. Had you been in on David and Abigail's "discussion" of the famine remedy, with which of the two would you have sided?

3. How might Yaconelli's outlook on the fear of God alter your approach, your mindset, as you go to church next Sunday morning?

4. Christ's death on the cross reconciles us to the God who is holy. Does that mean we no longer have to fear him?

5. Is there a link between indifference to the fear of God and Jesus' statement that few would be saved (the "narrow gate" of Matthew 7:14) and that false prophets may deceive even the elect (Matthew 24:24)?

2. David's pivotal part in God's redemptive plan.

From the beginning of time, God had a plan. From our viewpoint in history, we see the outline of that plan far clearer than the folks back then (i.e., Adam and Eve as they were being tossed out of the Garden, or Jeremiah sinking in the muck at the bottom of the well). The Word was there, however, and the plan had already been set in motion.

- Adam and Eve – Genesis 3, especially vs. 5.
- Noah and the flood – Genesis 6–9, especially 6:18 and 9:12 (God's covenant with Noah).
- Abraham, father of a chosen nation – Genesis 12:2–3, 7.
- The patriarchs and seed-bearers Isaac and Jacob – Genesis 25:19–26; Romans 9:7; Genesis 22:18.
- Joseph in Egypt – Genesis 39-47, especially 45:7.

- Moses and the Exodus – the entire book of Exodus; also Deuteronomy 18:15, 18–19, and Hebrews 11:25–27.
- Joshua claiming much of the Promised Land – Joshua 24, especially vs. 15.
- Judges – moral degeneracy and the deliverers God raised up. Note the final verse of the book.
- Desire for a king; Samuel's resistance – 1 Samuel 8:5–22.
- The Saul debacle – 1 Samuel 15, especially vss. 22–23.
- David:
    - Had a clear vision of Israel's holy destiny.
    - Accepted the covenant God offered him.
    - Finished establishing the kingdom that Moses and Joshua failed to complete.
    - Ruled as High King of the entire monarchy.
    - Looked beyond to a Redeemer yet to come.

Reflect on the following Scriptures. Although they do not speak of David, they show the outworking of God's plan, in which David played a strategic part.

- "But when the _time had fully come_, God sent his Son...."[93]
- "But now a _righteousness_ from God, apart from law, _has been made known_, to which the Law and the Prophets testify. This righteousness from God comes through faith in Jesus Christ to all who believe."[94]
- "Repent, then, and turn to God, so that your sins may be wiped out, that times of refreshing may come from the Lord, and that he may send the Christ, who has been _appointed for you_—even Jesus."[95]

---

93. Galatians 4:4, emphasis added.
94. Romans 3:21–22, emphasis added.
95. Acts 3:19–20, emphasis added.

- "*Salvation is found in no one else, for there is no other name under heaven given to men by which we must be saved.*"[96]
- "*For he chose us in him before the creation of the world to be holy and blameless in his sight. In love he predestined us to be adopted as his sons through Jesus Christ....*"[97]
- "*But when the kindness and love of God our Savior appeared, he saved us, not because of righteous things we had done, but because of his mercy.*"[98]
- "*In the past God spoke to our forefathers through the prophets at many times and in various ways, but in these last days he has spoken to us by his Son, whom he appointed heir of all things, and through whom he made the universe.*"[99]

3. David as a key figure in the Old Testament Messianic thread.

From the very beginning, God had great plans for David. Even before Samuel anointed the boy, God rebuked Saul through Samuel:

> You have not kept the command the LORD your God gave you; if you had, he would have established your kingdom over Israel for all time. But now your kingdom will not endure; the LORD has sought out a man after his own heart and appointed him leader of his people. (1 Samuel 13:13b–14)

A man after God's own heart? David? An adulterer...and a *murderer?*

In Scroll Three, chapter 24, Asaph reflects on a conversation he had had with David in which the grieving father asked why God couldn't have worked his will through Absalom as he had so obvi-

---

96. Acts 4:12, emphasis added.
97. Ephesians 1:4–5, emphasis added.
98. Titus 3:4–5, emphasis added.
99. Hebrews 1:1–2, emphasis added.

ously done through David. In the silence that follows, David sings
a psalm:

> Trust in the LORD and do good;
>   dwell in the land and enjoy safe pasture.
> Delight yourself in the LORD
>   and he will give you the desires of your
>   heart.[100]

Asaph thinks about this. "This tiny act of worship sketched in
clear, deft strokes the vast difference between father and son. The
poignancy of the moment tore my soul."

David knew how to repent; Absalom did not. David's heart passion centered on God; Absalom erected a monument to himself.

Thus, the word God gave to David:

> I took you from the pasture and from following the flock to be
> ruler over my people Israel. I have been with you wherever
> you have gone, and I have cut off all your enemies from before
> you. Now I will make your name great, like the names of the
> greatest men of the earth....The LORD declares to you that
> the LORD himself will establish a house for you: When your
> days are over and you rest with your fathers, I will raise up
> your offspring to succeed you, who will come from your own
> body, and I will establish his kingdom. [101]

Psalm 132:11 picks this up. "The LORD swore an oath to David, a
sure oath that he will not revoke: 'One of your own descendants I will
place on your throne.'" In this psalm, the worship of God is somehow
linked to the man who sits the earthly throne—not as a person to
be worshiped, but as a seed-carrier for the King who is to come.
Isaiah adds,

> A shoot will come up from the stump of Jesse; from his roots
> a Branch will bear fruit. The Spirit of the LORD will rest on
> him—

---

100. Psalm 37:3–4
101. 2 Samuel 7:8–12

> the Spirit of wisdom and of
>   understanding,
>
> the Spirit of counsel and of power,
>
> the Spirit of knowledge and of the fear of
>   the LORD—
>
> and he will delight in the fear of the
>   LORD.[102]

Jeremiah 23:5–6 says:

> "The days are coming," declares the LORD, "when I will raise
> up to David a righteous Branch, a King who will reign wisely
> and do what is just and right in the land. In his days Judah
> will be saved and Israel will live in safety. This is the name by
> which he will be called: The LORD Our Righteousness."
>
> Blessed is the coming kingdom of our father David! Hosanna
> in the highest!   (Mark 11:10)

And how clear and pointed can you get?

> I, Jesus, have sent my angel to give you this testimony for the
> churches. I am the Root and the Offspring of David, and the
> bright Morning Star."   (Revelation 22:16)

In the final chapter of *The Stones*, I gave David eyes to see this
King that is him but not him. "My son...yet somehow my Lord,"
he says.[103]

Jesus—Alpha and Omega, Mighty God, the Holy One who is to
be feared, and yet...and yet... "This king," says David, "wears the
face of love. *Yahweh* knows me, everything about me, yet...*loves me
still.* Asaph, what can I do? What can I say? Who can bear such
love?"

Who of us, indeed?

---

102. Isaiah 11:1–3

103. See Psalm 110, one of the most directly messianic passages of the Old
Testament.

Think for a moment:

1. Discuss ways in which *The Stones* has affected:
   - Your understanding of David and his place in Scripture.
   - Your devotional life.
   - Your relationship with God through Jesus Christ.
2. I can state unambiguously that writing *The Stones* has dramatically impacted my own heart and my mind. My deep desire is to stand alongside David in his passion for God.

   One thing I ask of the Lord,
   this is what I seek:
   that I may dwell in the house of the Lord
      all the days of my life,
      to gaze upon the beauty of the Lord
      and to seek him in his temple.
   For in the day of trouble
      he will keep me safe in his dwelling;
      he will hide me in the shelter of his tabernacle
      and set me high upon a rock.[104]

May you, too, come under the transforming influence of this man whose feet were clay, but heart was gold.

---

104. Psalm 27:4–5

About the Author

Eleanor K. Gustafson has been publishing both fiction and non-fiction since 1978. Her short stories and articles have appeared in a number of national and local magazines. *The Stones* is her fourth novel.

In many of her stories, Eleanor explores the cosmic struggle between good and evil in light of God's overarching work of redemption. A graduate of Wheaton College in Illinois, she has been actively involved in church life as a minister's wife, teacher, musician, writer, and encourager. She has enjoyed a variety of experiences, from horses to house building, all of which have helped bring color and humor to her fiction.

She and her husband live in Massachusetts, where he teaches philosophy. They travel extensively, spend time with their three children and eight grandchildren, and enjoy camping at the family forest in Chester, Vermont.

Breinigsville, PA USA
02 April 2010
235452BV00005B/18/P